Butterfly Spotting Handbook

PAUL DUFFIELD

CONTENTS

INTRODUCTION

This book is an all-in-one guide to butterfly spotting and contains details of the primary species of butterflies currently found in Britain.

Fact sheets are provided with full colour illustrations of each butterfly and maps of Britain showing where the different species of butterflies are found.

Details of size, conservation priority and preferred habitat are also provided, together with information to aid identification and differentiate between similar species.

Butterfly spotting is an enjoyable and rewarding activity that can be enjoyed by anyone, whether in town parks, gardens or on trips to the countryside or the beach.

With the information in this book you will be able to identify the butterflies you see and know where to look for the more elusive species.

THE SPECIES OF BUTTERFLIES FOUND IN BRITAIN

The species of butterfly currently found in Britain are divided into the family groups shown below.

HESPERIIDAE (SKIPPERS)   PAPILIONIDAE (SWALLOWTAILS)

Chequered skipper

Dingy skipper

Essex skipper

Swallowtail

Grizzled skipper

Large skipper

Lulworth skipper

Silver-spotted skipper

Small skipper

PIERIDAE (WHITES)

Brimstone

Clouded Yellow

Green-veined white

Large white

Orange-tip

Pale clouded yellow

Small white

Wood white

LYCAENIDAE (HAIRSTREAKS, COPPERS AND BLUES)

Adonis blue

Black hairstreak

Brown argus

Brown hairstreak

Chalkhill blue

Common blue

Duke of Burgundy

Green hairstreak

Holly blue

Large blue

Northern brown argus

Purple hairstreak

Silver-studded blue

Small blue

Small copper

White-letter hairstreak

NYMPHALIDAE (ARISTROCRATS, FRITILLARIES AND BROWNS)

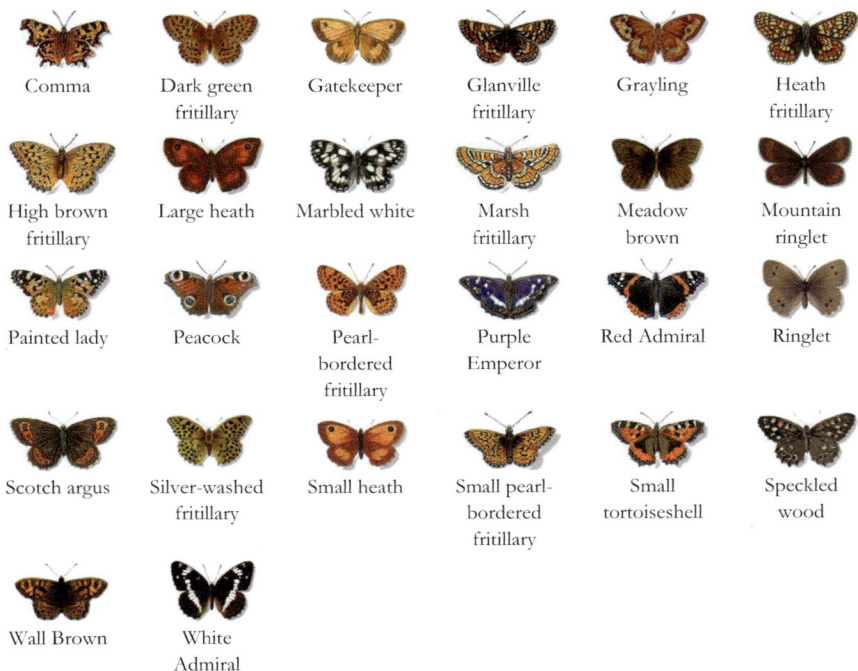

Comma	Dark green fritillary	Gatekeeper	Glanville fritillary	Grayling	Heath fritillary
High brown fritillary	Large heath	Marbled white	Marsh fritillary	Meadow brown	Mountain ringlet
Painted lady	Peacock	Pearl-bordered fritillary	Purple Emperor	Red Admiral	Ringlet
Scotch argus	Silver-washed fritillary	Small heath	Small pearl-bordered fritillary	Small tortoiseshell	Speckled wood
Wall Brown	White Admiral				

Fact sheets containing larger illustrations and information about each species are organised alphabetically within these family groups in the reference section towards the end of this book.

To find information about a particular butterfly, first identify the family group, then turn to the relevant section which starts on the page indicated below:

WHERE CAN YOU SPOT BUTTERFLIES?

Butterflies are all around us and can be seen almost anywhere. Common species can be found in town parks and gardens, while other species favour countryside habitats and may only be seen in woodland or coastal areas.

Not all species of butterfly are found all over Britain. Some species are only present in some, or even only one area, but most areas that are host to butterflies will have a variety of species for you to observe and identify.

Local wildlife groups and trusts often provide information on butterflies that can be seen in particular areas such as nature reserves and provide downloadable fact sheets on their websites containing suggested places to visit to spot butterflies.

A good place to find locations for butterfly spotting is the website of your local wildlife trust. The UK Wildlife Trusts cover regions of the United Kingdom, Isle of Man and Alderney and branches of the Irish Wildlife Trust cover regions of Ireland.

The UK Wildlife Trusts website is at: http://www.wildlifetrusts.org/.

The Irish Wildlife Trust website is at: http://iwt.ie/.

WHAT EQUIPMENT DO YOU NEED?

You can, of course, enjoy a day's butterfly spotting without any specialist equipment at all, but if you want to keep a record of the butterflies you spot, either for your own interest and enjoyment or so you can help with butterfly conservation efforts, it can help to take a few things with you.

Butterfly Spotting Guide

To assist with identification a guide with colour illustrations and descriptions, such as this book, will be useful. Alternatively you can download printable butterfly spotting sheets from websites such as the Big Butterfly Count at http://www.bigbutterflycount.org/ and Nature Detectives which is operated by the Woodland Trust at http://www.naturedetectives.org.uk/

You may also be able to download butterfly spotting sheets for particular locations such as the sheet made available by the National Trust at http://www.nationaltrust.org.uk/dyrham-park/wildlife/ for their Dyrham Park property.

If you are visiting an area with children, these sheets are all you need for a fun butterfly spotting competition to keep them entertained.

Binoculars

Binoculars are not essential, but can help you to pick out distinguishing characteristics of butterflies that are not close enough for detailed inspection.

Any pair of binoculars will help, but a pair described as 'close focus' will be better for picking out details such as marks or spots in wing patterns.

Notepad and Pencil

A notepad and pencil is useful for recording the species of butterflies you see, and for sketching and recording patterns and markings that you can use later if you are unable to immediately identify a butterfly.

If you intend to take part in a conservation monitoring scheme, a notepad is useful to record information that you can later collate and submit to the scheme.

Digital Camera

Pictures taken with a digital camera or camera-equipped mobile phone can be used to keep a record of the butterflies you spot and can also be useful to refer to later if you are not able to identify a butterfly you see.

If possible, try to photograph both the upper and lower wings so you have as much information as possible to help with later identification. This may mean that you need to take photographs of a butterfly both in flight and at rest to capture all possible detail.

HOW TO IDENTIFY THE BUTTERFLIES YOU SPOT

Many species of butterfly are similar in appearance and it can be difficult to tell one species from another without detailed examination.

There are, though, distinguishing characteristics that you can look for and if you use these, together with the pictures in this book, you should be able to make a positive identification.

Butterflies will rarely stay in one place long enough for you to compare them to several pictures so you may need to record information that you can examine in more detail later.

If you are able to take a photograph or two, or sketch the patterns of the upper and lower sides of the wings you will usually capture enough information to be reasonably confident which species you have seen.

If you are unsure of the identification of a butterfly you have seen, first try to narrow it down to similar looking species using the pictures in this book.

When you have a short-list, which will usually be of at most three or four potential matches, examine the wings for distinguishing characteristics. These are described on the pages for each species.

Often a single feature, such as an eye-like spot on the top of the wing can be used to tell one species from another, for example, the gatekeeper and the hedge brown are similar in appearance, but the large spot on the forewing of the gatekeeper contains two white marks, while that on the hedge brown has only one.

Sometimes it is necessary to examine the markings on the undersides of the wings to differentiate between species. A photograph or sketch of the butterfly at rest with the wings closed will aid identification.

If you are unable to positively identify a butterfly from its physical characteristics, additional information such as its size and the area of Britain or the type of habitat in which it was observed can provide additional clues.

Here are some examples of similar butterflies and how you can use individual characteristics to differentiate between them.

Essex skipper and small skipper

Essex skipper   **Small skipper**

The Essex skipper and small skipper are almost identical in appearance, but can be differentiated by examining the tips of the antennae.

The tips of the antennae on the Essex skipper are black and shiny while those of the small skipper are lighter in colour.

Gatekeeper and female meadow brown

Gatekeeper   **Meadow brown**

The similar gatekeeper and female meadow brown can be differentiated by examining the eye-like spots at the front of the forewings.

The spots on the gatekeeper have two white marks while those on the meadow brown have only one.

HESPERIIDAE (SKIPPERS)

Hesperiidae, known as Skippers are small butterflies with short plump bodies and hooked antennae. Most are primarily orange or brown in colour.

Skippers are so named because of the quick darting flight that is characteristic of this species.

Wings are usually well rounded with sharper tipped fore wings, the wings being smaller in proportion to their bodies that other species of butterfly.

Skippers occur worldwide with more than 3,500 recognised species. There are 8 species of skippers currently found in Britain.

Chequered skipper

Dingy skipper

Essex skipper

Grizzled skipper

Large skipper

Lulworth skipper

Silver-spotted skipper

Small skipper

CHEQUERED SKIPPER

Scientific name:
Carterocephalus palaemon

Typical wingspan: 30mm

Conservation priority: High

Description:

A small fast flying butterfly with a brown and gold check pattern on the wings.

Habitat:

Grassland on the edges of open broadleaf woodland.

Locations:

Extinct in England since the mid 1970s but still found in western Scotland.

DINGY SKIPPER

Scientific name:
Erynnis tages

Typical wingspan: 29mm

Conservation priority: High

Description:

A small butterfly with a drab grey and brown pattern on the wings.

Habitat:

Woodland clearings, coastal dunes, and chalk downs.

Locations:

Found throughout Britain but distribution is patchy.

ESSEX SKIPPER

Scientific name:
Thymelicus lineola

Typical wingspan: 29mm

Conservation priority: Low

Description:

A small butterfly with bright orange/brown wings. Almost identical to the small skipper, but identifiable by black tips to the antennae which on the small skipper are lighter in colour.

Habitat:

Dry grassland in open sunny areas, roadside verges, woodlands and coastal marshland.

Locations:

Widely distributed in central and southern England.

GRIZZLED SKIPPER

Scientific name:
Pyrgus malvae

Typical wingspan: 27mm

Conservation priority: High

Description:

A small butterfly with a black and white check pattern on the outer parts of the wings.

Habitat:

Wood clearings, chalk downland and scrub grassland.

Locations:

Found throughout southern and central England and Wales, but has declined in several areas.

LARGE SKIPPER

Scientific name:
Ochlodes sylvanus

Typical wingspan: 34mm

Conservation priority: Low

Description:

A small butterfly with brown edged orange wings and pale orange spots.

Habitat:

Hedgerows, woodland clearings and areas of tall grassland.

Locations:

England, Wales and south west Scotland.

LULWORTH SKIPPER

Male:

Female:

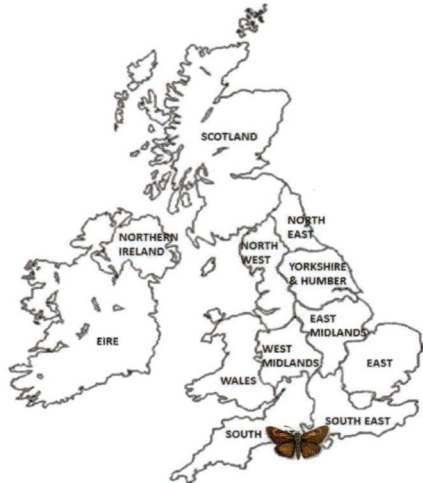

Scientific name:
Thymelicus acteon

Typical wingspan: 26mm

Conservation priority: High

Description:

A small butterfly with dull orange/brown wings. Females are similar to the male but lighter in colour.

Habitat:

Sheltered or south facing slopes of chalk downland and coastal grassland.

Locations:

Mainly restricted to the south Dorset coast.

SILVER-SPOTTED SKIPPER

Scientific name:
Hesperia comma

Typical wingspan: 33mm

Conservation priority: Medium

Description:

A small butterfly with brown edged orange wings and pale orange spots. Distinguishable from other skippers by silver spots on the underside of the wings.

Habitat:

Areas of chalk downland.

Locations:

Southern England, mainly found in Dorset, Hampshire and Wiltshire.

SMALL SKIPPER

Scientific name:
Thymelicus sylvestris

Typical wingspan: 30mm

Conservation priority: Low

Description:

A small butterfly with bright orange/brown wings. Almost identical to the Essex skipper, but identifiable by light coloured tips to the antennae which on the Essex skipper are black.

Habitat:

Open areas of rough grassland, road verges, edges of fields and woodlands.

Locations:

Widely distributed in Britain up to North Yorkshire and the border of Scotland.

PAPILIONIDAE (SWALLOWTAILS)

Papilionidae, known as swallowtails are large colourful butterflies.

 Most swallowtails are tropical species, but members of this family are present throughout the world.

Only one species of Papilionidae is found in Britain and is restricted to areas of the Norfolk broads.

Swallowtail

SWALLOWTAIL

Scientific name:
Papilio machaon

Typical wingspan: 85mm

Conservation priority: Medium

Description:

A large black veined butterfly, pale in the centre, blue at the edges, with a red spot at the back of the wing.

Habitat:

Areas of fen vegetation in the Norfolk Broads.

Locations:

Norfolk Broads. Rarely, but occasionally, seen in other parts of Britain.

PIERIDAE (WHITES)

Pieridae, known as whites are mostly white, yellow or orange in coloration, often displaying black spots.

There are over 1,000 species of Pieridae, most of which are tropical species in Africa and Asia.

In Britain, species of Pieridae range in size from the large white with a typical wingspan of 67mm to the much smaller wood white which has a typical wingspan of 42mm.

Currently 8 species of Pieridae are found in Britain.

Brimstone

Clouded Yellow

Green-veined white

Large white

Orange-tip

Pale clouded yellow

Small white

Wood white

BRIMSTONE

Scientific name:
Gonepteryx rhamni

Typical wingspan: 60mm

Conservation priority: Low

Description:

A large leaf shaped butterfly with yellow wings. Females are similar to the male, but lighter in colour.

Habitat:

Scrubby grassland and woodland and is often seen near hedgerows and roadside verges.

Locations:

Throughout central and southern England and parts of Ireland.

CLOUDED YELLOW

Scientific name:
Colias croceus

Typical wingspan: 60mm

Conservation priority: N/A

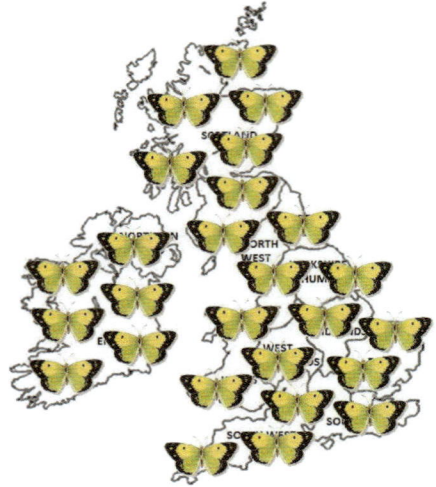

Description:

A large butterfly with yellow wings bordered black. A black spot is present at the front of each wing and two silver white spots at the back.

Habitat:

Flowered areas, especially unimproved chalk downlands.

Locations:

Widely distributed in Britain and especially common near the coasts of southern England.

GREEN-VEINED WHITE

Scientific name:
Pieris napi

Typical wingspan: 50mm

Conservation priority: Low

Description:

A medium sized butterfly with green veined white wings and dark spots on the upper wings.

Habitat:

Damp areas of vegetation in meadows, moorland, woods and near lakes, rivers and ponds.

Locations:

Widespread throughout Britain.

LARGE WHITE

Male:

Female:

Scientific name:
Pieris brassicae

Typical wingspan: 67mm

Conservation priority: Low

Description:

A large strong flying butterfly with bright white wings. Both male and female have black edged forewings, females also have black spots on the forewings.

Habitat:

Wide range of areas, especially allotments and gardens where cabbages are cultivated.

Locations:

Widespread throughout Britain.

ORANGE-TIP

Male:

Female:

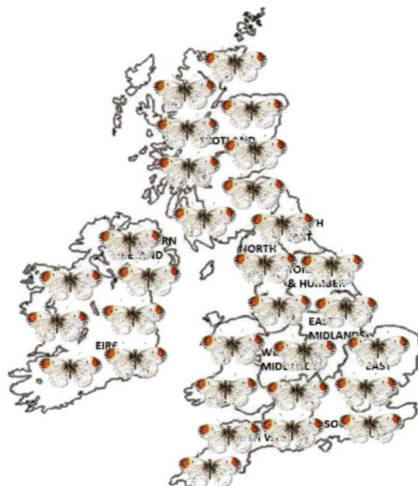

Scientific name:
Anthocharis cardamines

Typical wingspan: 48mm

Conservation priority: Low

Description:

A medium sized butterfly with white wings. Forewings are bordered black, males having an orange tip which is not present on the female.

Habitat:

Damp areas of woodland glades, hedgerows, meadows and the banks of streams and rivers.

Locations:

Widespread throughout Britain.

PALE CLOUDED YELLOW

Scientific name:
Colias hyale

Typical wingspan: 55mm

Conservation priority: N/A

Description:

A large butterfly with pale yellow wings bordered black. A black spot is present at the front of each wing.

Habitat:

Coastal cliffs and open downland.

Locations:

A rare visitor to Britain, occasionally sighted in the south of England and Ireland.

SMALL WHITE

Scientific name:
Pieris rapae

Typical wingspan: 48mm

Conservation priority: Low

Description:

A medium sized butterfly with bright white wings. Forewings are tipped black and have dark spots.

Habitat:

Wide range of areas, especially allotments and gardens where cabbages are cultivated.

Locations:

Widespread throughout Britain.

WOOD WHITE

Scientific name:
Leptidea sinapis

Typical wingspan: 42mm

Conservation priority: Low

Description:

A small slow flying butterfly with rounded wings and black tipped forewings.

Habitat:

Areas of grassland in woodland clearings and some coastal cliffs.

Locations:

Central and southern England and parts of Ireland.

LYCAENIDAE (HAIRSTREAKS, COPPERS AND BLUES)

Lycaenidae, known as hairstreaks, coppers and blues are small and brightly

coloured butterflies, some species having a metallic sheen.

With over 5,000 species worldwide, Lycaenidae is the second largest family of butterflies and includes some of the smallest butterflies in the world.

Currently, 16 species of Lycaenidae are found in Britain.

Adonis blue	Black hairstreak	Brown argus
Brown hairstreak	Chalkhill blue	Common blue
Duke of Burgundy	Green hairstreak	Holly blue
Large blue	Northern brown argus	Purple hairstreak
Silver-studded blue	Small blue	Small copper
White-letter hairstreak		

ADONIS BLUE

Male:

Female:

Scientific name:
Lysandra bellargus

Typical wingspan: 38mm

Conservation priority: Medium

Description:

A small/medium sized butterfly. Males have bright sky blue wings, females brown. Wings are edged white, crossed by black lines.

Habitat:

South facing slopes in grassland areas of chalk or limestone.

Locations:

Dorset, Wiltshire, Sussex and Kent.

BLACK HAIRSTREAK

Male:

Female:

Scientific name:
Satyrium pruni

Typical wingspan: 37mm

Conservation priority: High

Description:

A small/medium sized butterfly, primarily dark brown in colour with an orange pattern on the outer edges of the wings, more pronounced on the female.

Habitat:

Woodland glades and hedgerows in areas densely populated with Blackthorn.

Locations:

Rare and only found in Oxfordshire and Cambridgeshire.

BROWN ARGUS

Scientific name:
Aricia agestis

Typical wingspan: 29mm

Conservation priority: Low

Description:

A small butterfly with brown wings edged with a row of orange spots.

Habitat:

Areas of chalk and limestone grassland, coastal dunes, heathland and woodland clearings.

Locations:

Widespread in central and southern England and the coast of Wales.

BROWN HAIRSTREAK

Male:

Female:

Scientific name:

Thecla betulae

Typical wingspan: 39mm

Conservation priority: High

Description:

A small medium sized butterfly with brown wings. Females have a large orange/yellow spot on the upper wings which may also be present on the male but is much less pronounced.

Habitat:

Areas of blackthorn hedges, scrub and edges of woodland.

Locations:

Mostly found in south west Wales, Surrey, Sussex, Devon and Cornwall.

CHALKHILL BLUE

Male:

Female:

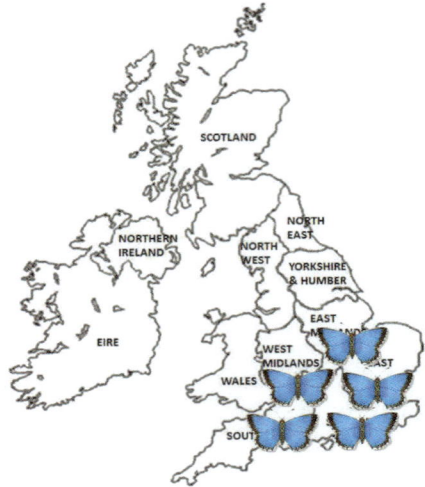

Scientific name:

Lysandra coridon

Typical wingspan: 38mm

Conservation priority: Medium

Description:

A small medium sized butterfly. Males have light blue wings, bordered brown with a thin white edge. Females are brown with orange spots on the edges of the wings.

Habitat:

limestone and chalk grassland areas.

Locations:

Mostly found in southern England.

COMMON BLUE

Male:

Female:

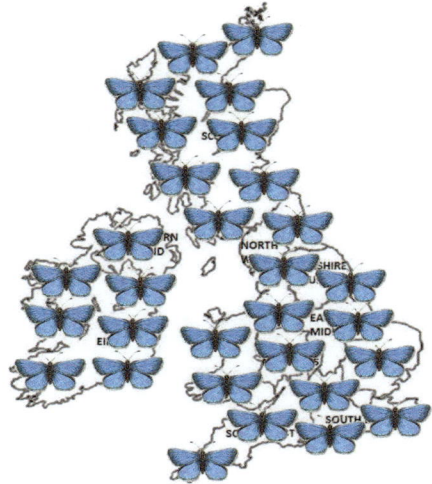

Scientific name:
Polyommatus icarus

Typical wingspan: 35mm

Conservation priority: Low

Description:

A small butterfly with blue wings, bordered black with a thin blue/white edge. Females vary in colour from brown blue with hints of brown.

Habitat:

Coastal dunes, road verges, woodland clearings, areas of waste ground and open uncultivated areas such as disused quarries.

Locations:

Widespread throughout Britain.

DUKE OF BURGUNDY

Scientific name:
Hamearis lucina

Typical wingspan: 30mm

Conservation priority: High

Description:

A small butterfly with an orange and brown pattern. Undersides of the rear wings have rows of white spots.

Habitat:

Limestone and chalk grassland areas and woodland clearings.

Locations:

Mostly found in central southern England but small populations exist in other areas.

GREEN HAIRSTREAK

Scientific name:
Callophrys rubi

Typical wingspan: 33mm

Conservation priority: Medium

Description:

A small butterfly with green wings. The green colour is more pronounced on the underside of the wings and has a metallic sheen.

Habitat:

Chalk grassland, woodland clearings, heaths, moors and boggy areas.

Locations:

Widespread throughout Britain.

HOLLY BLUE

Male:

Female:

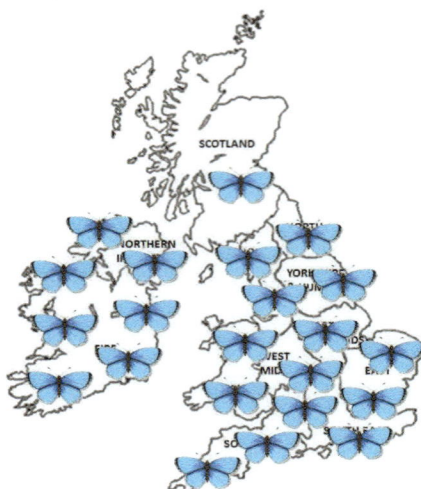

Scientific name:
Celastrina argiolus

Typical wingspan: 35mm

Conservation priority: Low

Description:

A small bright blue butterfly with a black border around the wing edges. This border is much more pronounced in the female. The undersides of the wings are pale blue with dark spots.

Habitat:

Hedgerows and woodlands as well as urban areas such as parks and gardens.

Locations:

Widespread in England and Wales with some populations in Ireland and Scotland.

LARGE BLUE

Scientific name:
Maculinea arion

Typical wingspan: 41mm

Conservation priority: High

Description:

A small/medium sized butterfly, larger than other blues. Wings are blue in colour with a darker border and a pattern of black spots.

Habitat:

Coastal and limestone grassland areas.

Locations:

Very rare in Britain, currently found only in south west England where it has been reintroduced by conservation groups.

NORTHERN BROWN ARGUS

Scientific name:
Aricia artaxerxes

Typical wingspan: 29mm

Conservation priority: High

Description:

A small butterfly with brown wings edged with rows of orange spots. Some individuals also have a white spot on the forewings.

Habitat:

Grassland areas of sand dunes, coastal valleys and quarries.

Locations:

Scotland and northern counties of England.

PURPLE HAIRSTREAK

Male:

Female:

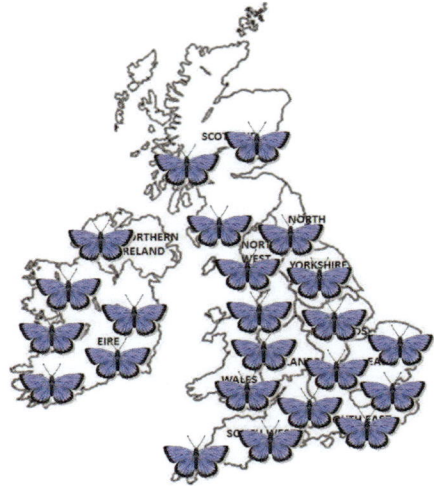

Scientific name:
Neozephyrus quercus

Typical wingspan: 38mm

Conservation priority: Low

Description:

A small butterfly with brown wings that have a purple sheen on the male, and purple markings on the forewings of the female.

Habitat:

Woodlands, hedgerows and areas of parkland.

Locations:

Widespread in England and Wales with some populations in Scotland and Ireland.

SILVER-STUDDED BLUE

Male:

Female:

Scientific name:
Plebejus argus

Typical wingspan: 30mm

Conservation priority: Medium

Description:

A small butterfly, males with blue wings edged with a dark border, females with brown wings edged with rows of orange spots. The undersides of the wings are brown/grey with black and orange spots flecked green at the outer edges.

Habitat:

Chalk and limestone grassland, heaths and sand dunes.

Locations:

North Wales and counties of southern England.

SMALL BLUE

Scientific name:
Cupido minimus

Typical wingspan: 29mm

Conservation priority: Medium

Description:

A small butterfly, smaller than other blues, with brown wings dusted blue. The undersides of the wings are pale blue with a row of black spots.

Habitat:

Chalk and limestone grassland, dunes, quarries and embankments.

Locations:

Mainly found in south central England with some populations on the coasts of Ireland and Scotland.

SMALL COPPER

Scientific name:
Lycaena phlaeas

Typical wingspan: 33mm

Conservation priority: Low

Description:

A small bright copper coloured butterfly with brown spots and brown wing edges. The undersides of the wings are orange/brown with dark spots.

Habitat:

Chalk grassland, woodland clearings, heaths, waste ground and moorland.

Locations:

Widespread throughout Britain except uplands of northern Britain.

WHITE-LETTER HAIRSTREAK

Scientific name:
Satyrium w-album

Typical wingspan: 36mm

Conservation priority: High

Description:

A small/medium sized butterfly with brown wings. The undersides of the wings are brown with a white W shaped streak and an orange border.

Habitat:

Hedgerows, woodlands and areas of mixed scrub.

Locations:

Widespread in England and Wales but less common in far western areas.

NYMPHALIDAE (ARISTROCRATS, FRITILLARIES AND BROWNS)

Nymphalidae, known as aristocrats, fritillaries and browns are medium to large sized butterflies

With over 6.000 species worldwide, Nymphalidae is the larges family of butterflies.

This family contains many of the largest and most brightly coloured butterflies in Britain, including the emperors, admirals and fritillaries.

There are currently 26 species of Nymphalidae found in Britain.

Comma	Dark green fritillary	Gatekeeper	Glanville fritillary	Grayling	Heath fritillary
High brown fritillary	Large heath	Marbled white	Marsh fritillary	Meadow brown	Mountain ringlet
Painted lady	Peacock	Pearl-bordered fritillary	Purple Emperor	Red Admiral	Ringlet
Scotch argus	Silver-washed fritillary	Small heath	Small pearl-bordered fritillary	Small tortoiseshell	Speckled wood
Wall Brown	White Admiral				

COMMA

Scientific name:
Polygonia c-album

Typical wingspan: 57mm

Conservation priority: Low

Description:

A medium sized butterfly with a distinctive ragged wing marked in orange and brown. The undersides of the wings are brown with a white mark shaped like a comma.

Habitat:

Edges and open areas of woodland and often seen in gardens.

Locations:

Widespread in England and Wales, some populations also found in Scotland and Ireland.

DARK GREEN FRITILLARY

Scientific name:
Argynnis aglaja

Typical wingspan: 66mm

Conservation priority: Medium

Description:

A large powerful butterfly with orange wings marked with a pattern of black lines and spots. Similar to the high brown fritillary from which it can be distinguished by an extra row of orange ringed marks on the underside of the wings that are not present on the dark green fritillary.

Habitat:

Limestone and chalk grassland, coastal dunes, moorlands and woodland clearings.

Locations:

Found throughout Britain but less common in eastern areas.

GATEKEEPER

Scientific name:
Pyronia tithonus

Typical wingspan: 43mm

Conservation priority: Low

Description:

A medium sized butterfly. Wings are orange with a dark border and black eye-like spots on the forewings. Distinguishable from the similar meadow brown by two white marks on these spots, while the meadow brown has only one.

Habitat:

Hedgerows, woodlands and heaths.

Locations:

Found in southern counties of England, Wales and the far south of Ireland.

GLANVILLE FRITILLARY

Scientific name:
Melitaea cinxia

Typical wingspan: 44mm

Conservation priority: High

Description:

A small/medium sized butterfly with an orange and brown chequered pattern on the wings and a pattern of cream and orange bands with black marks on the undersides of the wings.

Habitat:

Coastal grassland, areas of chalk downland and woodland clearings.

Locations:

Populations are restricted to the Isle of Wight.

GRAYLING

Scientific name:
Hipparchia semele

Typical wingspan: 58mm

Conservation priority: High

Description:

A medium/large sized butterfly with brown wings and dark spots contained in a lighter border at the edges of the wings. The undersides of the wings are mottled brown.

Habitat:

Chalk grassland, woodlands, dry areas of heaths, disused quarries and derelict industrial sites.

Locations:

Found throughout Britain mainly in coastal areas.

HEATH FRITILLARY

Scientific name:
Melitaea athalia

Typical wingspan: 48mm

Conservation priority: High

Description:

A small/medium sized butterfly with dusky brown and orange patterned wings.

Habitat:

Woodlands and heathland valleys.

Locations:

A rare endangered species found only in areas of Cornwall, Devon, Essex and Kent.

HIGH BROWN FRITILLARY

Scientific name:
Argynnis adippe

Typical wingspan: 64mm

Conservation priority: High

Description:

A large powerful butterfly with orange wings marked by a pattern of black lines and spots. Similar to the dark green fritillary from which it can be distinguished by an extra row of orange ringed marks on the underside of the wings that are not present on the dark green fritillary.

Habitat:

Areas of grass and bracken and rocky limestone outcrops.

Locations:

A highly endangered species found in very few areas of England and Wales.

LARGE HEATH

Scientific name:
Coenonympha tullia

Typical wingspan: 41mm

Conservation priority: High

Description:

A small/medium sized butterfly with brown wings, darker at the edges and with a large eye-like spot at the front of the forewings.

Habitat:

Wet areas of heathland, moorland and bogs.

Locations:

Mostly found in northern areas of Britain and Ireland, but some populations exist in other areas.

MARBLED WHITE

Scientific name:
Melanargia galathea

Typical wingspan: 56mm

Conservation priority: Low

Description:

A medium sized butterfly with a black and white checked pattern on the wings.

Habitat:

Chalk and limestone grassland, coastal grassland, woodland clearings, verges and embankments.

Locations:

Southern and central England and south Wales.

MARSH FRITILLARY

Scientific name:
Euphydryas aurinia

Typical wingspan: 45mm

Conservation priority: High

Description:

A medium sized butterfly with a bright orange and yellow check pattern on the wings.

Habitat:

Damp areas of grassland and woodland clearings.

Locations:

South west and central southern England, western areas of Wales and Scotland and Northern Ireland.

MEADOW BROWN

Male:

Female:

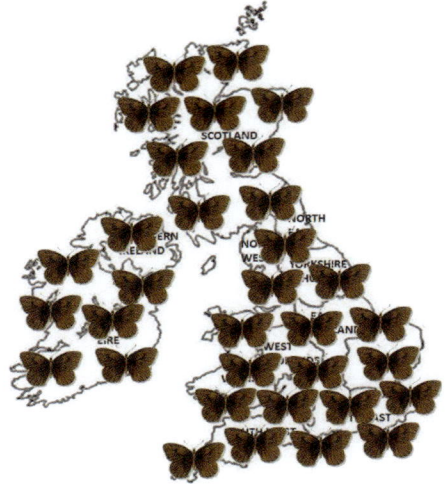

Scientific name:

Maniola jurtina

Typical wingspan: 53mm

Conservation priority: Low

Description:

A medium sized butterfly with brown wings and a black eye-like spot on the fore wings. Females and males are similar, but females are more brightly coloured. Can be distinguished from the similar gatekeeper by a single white mark on the spots, while the gatekeeper has two.

Habitat:

Coastal dunes, heaths, hay meadows, hedgerows, road verges and woodland clearings.

Locations:

Found throughout Britain.

MOUNTAIN RINGLET

Scientific name:
Erebia epiphron

Typical wingspan: 36mm

Conservation priority: High

Description:

A medium sized dark brown butterfly with a row of black-centred orange eye-like spots on the wings. Can be distinguished from the similar Scotch Argus which has white dots in the pots.

Habitat:

Damp areas of mountain grassland.

Locations:

Populations are restricted to mountain areas of central Scotland and the Lake District.

PAINTED LADY

Scientific name:
Vanessa cardui

Typical wingspan: 53mm

Conservation priority: Low

Description:

A medium sized butterfly with orange/brown wings marked with black and white spots on the forewings. The undersides of the wings are mottled brown with light bordered dark spots.

Habitat:

Dry open areas, often seen in large numbers in cultivated flowery areas of parks and gardens

Locations:

Widespread throughout Britain.

PEACOCK

Scientific name:
Inachis io

Typical wingspan: 66mm

Conservation priority: Low

Description:

A medium/large sized butterfly with distinctive large peacock-like spots on the fore wings and hind wings.

Habitat:

A wide range of habitats and often seen in cultivated areas of parks and gardens.

Locations:

Widespread throughout Britain.

PEARL-BORDERED FRITILLARY

Scientific name:
Boloria euphrosyne

Typical wingspan: 46mm

Conservation priority: High

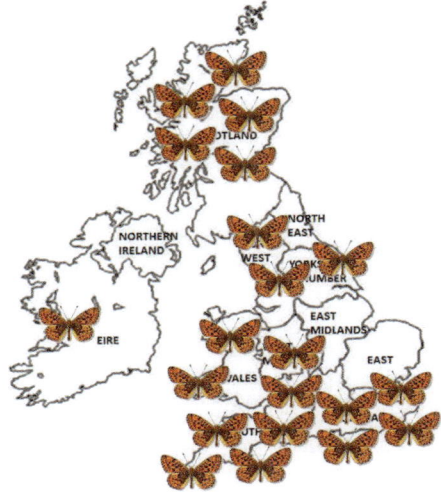

Description:

A medium sized butterfly with bright orange wings marked with a pattern of black lines and spots. Can be distinguished from the similar small pearl-bordered fritillary which has two large silver spots and a row of outer spots on the underside of the hind wing.

Habitat:

Areas of bracken and grass and woodland clearings.

Locations:

Widespread in northern Scotland, Cumbria, Devon, Cornwall and south east England.

PURPLE EMPEROR

Male:

Female:

Scientific name:

Apatura iris

Typical wingspan: 80mm

Conservation priority: Medium

Description:

A large butterfly with dark wings containing white bands and orange spots. While the male has a purple sheen, the wings of the female are predominately brown.

Habitat:

Areas of broadleaved woodland and Willow..

Locations:

Widespread in England and Wales with populations in areas of Scotland and Ireland.

RED ADMIRAL

Scientific name:

Vanessa atalanta

Typical wingspan: 70mm

Conservation priority: Low

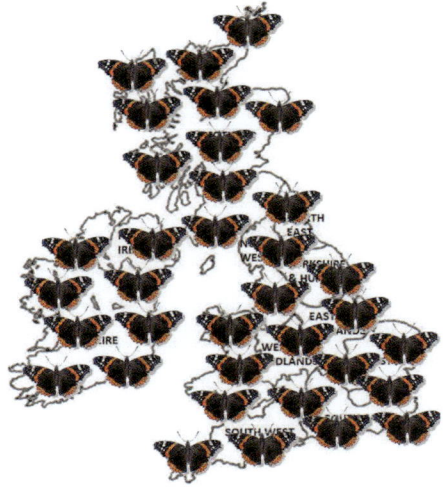

Description:

A large butterfly with black/dark brown wings with red bands and white spots near the tips of the fore wings. The undersides of the wings are dark and mottled.

Habitat:

A wide range of areas including gardens, coastal areas, towns and villages.

Locations:

Common throughout Britain.

RINGLET

Scientific name:
Aphantopus hyperantus

Typical wingspan: 50mm

Conservation priority: Low

Description:

A medium sized butterfly with mid-brown wings and darker spots. The undersides of the wings have several light bordered dark spots.

Habitat:

Areas of damp grassland, verges, riverbanks and woodland clearings.

Locations:

Found throughout Britain except northern Scotland.

SCOTCH ARGUS

Scientific name:
Erebia aethiops

Typical wingspan: 37mm

Conservation priority: Low

Description:

A medium sized butterfly with dark brown wings. A row of orange bordered black eye-like spots with white centres is present on each wing.

Habitat:

Limestone grassland, woodland clearings and boggy areas.

Locations:

Widespread in Scotland, some populations exist in areas of England.

SILVER-WASHED FRITILLARY

Scientific name:
Argynnis paphia

Typical wingspan: 74mm

Conservation priority: Low

Description:

A large fast flying butterfly with orange wings marked with a pattern of dark lines and spots. It can be distinguished from other fritillaries by pointed wings and silver streaks on the undersides of the wings.

Habitat:

Broadleaved and mixed woodland and hedgerows.

Locations:

Southern England and Wales and throughout Ireland.

SMALL HEATH

Scientific name:
Coenonympha pamphilus

Typical wingspan: 36mm

Conservation priority: High

Description:

A small butterfly with orange wings, darker at the edges and containing eye-like black spots.

Habitat:

Areas of dry, well drained grassland, woodland clearings, coastal dunes and road verges.

Locations:

Found throughout Britain.

SMALL PEARL-BORDERED FRITILLARY

Scientific name:
Boloria selene

Typical wingspan: 42mm

Conservation priority: High

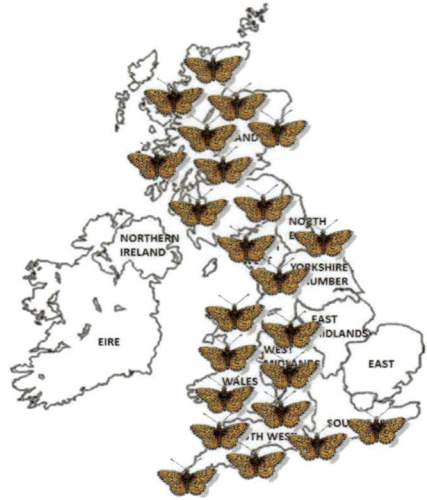

Description:

A medium sized butterfly with bright orange wings marked with a pattern of black lines and spots. Can be distinguished from the similar pearl-bordered fritillary by two large silver spots and a row of outer spots on the underside of its hind wing.

Habitat:

Areas of damp grassland, moorland, wood pasture and woodland clearings.

Locations:

Mainly found in western areas of Britain.

SMALL TORTOISESHELL

Scientific name:
Aglais urticae

Typical wingspan: 53mm

Conservation priority: Low

Description:

A medium/large sized butterfly with bright orange and black wings with a white spot near the edge of the fore wing.

Habitat:

A wide range of areas, often seen in cultivated flowery areas of parks and gardens.

Locations:

Found throughout Britain.

SPECKLED WOOD

Scientific name:
Pararge aegeria

Typical wingspan: 48mm

Conservation priority: Low

Description:

A medium sized butterfly with dark brown wings patterned with cream coloured patches on the wings.

Habitat:

Woodland clearings, hedgerows, parks and gardens.

Locations:

Found throughout all but far northern areas of England, Wales, Ireland and northern Scotland.

WALL BROWN

Scientific name:
Lasiommata megera

Typical wingspan: 45mm

Conservation priority: High

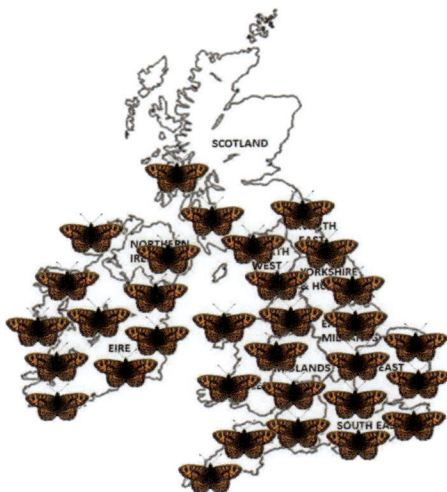

Description:

A medium sized butterfly with orange wings patterned with brown lines and spots. The undersides of the wings are delicately patterned in light shades of brown.

Habitat:

Areas of short grassland, coastal dunes, disused quarries, embankments and gardens.

Locations:

Widespread in England, Wales and Ireland.

WHITE ADMIRAL

Scientific name:
Limenitis camilla

Typical wingspan: 62mm

Conservation priority: High

Description:

A medium/large sized butterfly with black wings patterned with large white bands. The undersides of the wings are white with large brown bands containing dark spots.

Habitat:

Shaded areas of mature deciduous and mixed woodland.

Locations:

Restricted to areas of southern and central England.

THE STATE OF BUTTERFLIES IN BRITAIN

While Britain is host to almost 60 different species of butterflies, the number of species and population sizes of remaining species has been declining for many years.

Some species have disappeared completely and others are significantly at risk. If you would like to know about current conservation efforts to ensure the survival of declining species, you can find out more at the website of Butterfly Conservation: http://butterfly-conservation.org.

Butterfly Conservation and its partners have produced three State of Britain's/UK's Butterflies reports, which summarise the key results and conservation implications of recording and monitoring programs.

The most recent was published in 2011 highlighting the continuing decline of the UK's butterflies, measured by changes in distribution and population levels over a 10-year period.

The key findings of the report are that many butterfly species have continued to decline, over 70% of species having decreased in numbers and over 50% having decreased in distribution over the period of the report.

In all, three quarters of Britain's butterfly species have declined and while some threatened species have stabilised due to conservation efforts, more needs to be done to safeguard Britain's butterflies for the future.

If you would like to get involved in butterfly conservation you can find out how you can help at the Butterfly Conservation website.

There are many ways you can help; by contributing money towards conservation efforts; by taking part in monitoring programs that help to identify the butterfly populations at risk so conservation efforts can be targeted where they are most needed and by providing butterfly-friendly habitats in your own gardens.

ACKNOWLEDGMENTS

Images adapted from illustrations in 'Natural History of British Butterflies', James Duncan, 1840, 'Coleman's British Butterflies' W.S. Coleman, 1895 and 'A History of British Butterflies', Rev. Francis Orpen Morris, 1852.

ABOUT THE AUTHOR

Paul Duffield is an author with a keen interest in the countryside.

He became interested in nature at a young age and having lived, worked, fished and walked over many parts of Britain he became fascinated by the different birds, animals and insects that are found in countryside areas compared to those seen in towns.

A particular interest in the many different species of butterflies that he observed on his travels led to research into the butterflies of Britain and the compilation of this handbook.

Printed in Great Britain
by Amazon